Poet's Workshop

Read, Recite, and Write

LIST POEMS

Chickadees frolic
in the sprinkler, bathe
in puddles on the patio

The arched trellis, encased
in delicate cardinal vines
bright red star-shapes
sing hummingbird's song

Trees in full regalia
abs_____ for
shade and g_____

JoAnn Early Macken

POET'S WORKSHOP

Author
JoAnn Early Macken

Publishing plan research and development
Reagan Miller

Project coordinator
Kelly Spence

Editor
Anastasia Suen

Proofreader and indexer
Wendy Scavuzzo

Design
Margaret Amy Salter

Photo research
Margaret Amy Salter

Prepress technician
Margaret Amy Salter

Print and production coordinator
Margaret Amy Salter

Photographs and illustrations
All images by Shutterstock

JoAnn Early Macken is the author of *Write a Poem Step by Step* (Earlybird Press), five picture books, and 125 nonfiction books for young readers. Her poems appear in several children's magazines and anthologies. JoAnn has taught writing at four Wisconsin colleges. She speaks about poetry and writing to students, teachers, and adult writers at schools, libraries, and conferences. You can visit her web site at www.joannmacken.com.

Library and Archives Canada Cataloguing in Publication

Macken, JoAnn Early, 1953-, author
    Read, recite, and write list poems / JoAnn Early Macken.

(Poet's workshop)
Includes index.
Issued in print and electronic formats.
ISBN 978-0-7787-1965-6 (bound).--ISBN 978-0-7787-1969-4 (pbk.).--
ISBN 978-1-4271-7603-5 (pdf).--ISBN 978-1-4271-7599-1 (html)

    1. Poetry--Authorship--Juvenile literature. I. Title. II. Title:
List poems. III. Series: Macken, JoAnn Early, 1953- . Poet's
workshop.

PN1525.M33 2015   j808.1   C2014-908198-7
                                          C2014-908199-5

Library of Congress Cataloging-in-Publication Data

CIP available at Library of Congress

Crabtree Publishing Company

www.crabtreebooks.com 1-800-387-7650

Printed in Canada/042015/EF20150224

Published in Canada
Crabtree Publishing
616 Welland Ave.
St. Catharines, Ontario
L2M 5V6

Published in the United States
Crabtree Publishing
PMB 59051
350 Fifth Avenue, 59th Floor
New York, New York 10118

Published in the United Kingdom
Crabtree Publishing
Maritime House
Basin Road North, Hove
BN41 1WR

Published in Australia
Crabtree Publishing
3 Charles Street
Coburg North
VIC 3058

Contents

Chapter 1: What Is a List Poem?

A list has a purpose. It is a way to keep track of things. People make lists of goals. They list birds they see and tasks to do. They plan shopping trips. Most of these lists are not poems, however.

A list poem is more than just a list. It might include a comment that ties the items together. It might **evoke**, or stir up, a certain feeling. A comment can tell what the list items mean.

Like a list, a list poem can have a purpose. It can explain what connects things that seem to be different. A list poem can even tell a story. Different kinds of list poems have their own purposes.

A **biopoem** is a short **biography**, or life story. It introduces a person.

A **riddle poem** presents a puzzle to solve.

An **acrostic** spells out a word or **phrase**.

Read on to learn more about list poems.

Prose vs. Drama vs. Poetry

In literature, we use different names to talk about the way words are used. As you can see in the examples below, the same story can be told in many different ways.

Prose

Gems of many colors sparkle. Flint is a type of quartz. Strike it against steel. It creates sparks.

Drama

TIME: afternoon
PLACE: outside a jewelry store
STAGE DIRECTIONS: [points in the window]
GRANDPA: Precious stones are pretty. Flint is more useful. It can start a fire.

We use sentences to tell a story in **prose**. When a story is performed as a play, it is called **drama**. Can you see the stage directions? They let the actors know when and where things happen.

The third example is a poem. A **poem** uses short phrases to tell a story or share a feeling.

Poetry

Flint

An emerald is as green as grass,
A ruby red as blood;
A sapphire shines as blue as heaven;
A flint lies in the mud.
A diamond is a brilliant stone,
To catch the world's desire;
An opal holds a fiery spark;
But a flint holds fire.

—Christina Rossetti

Writing Your Own List Poem

A list poem is also called a **catalog poem**. To write one, begin with a list. Write down things that go together. The lines can be short or long. The items can be obvious, or they can be surprising. A list poem can be about anything. It's up to you!

A list of items is not a list poem—yet. What gives the list meaning? Why are the items important? How do you feel about them? Add a comment that ties the list items together.

Place the lines in the best order. You can make a point. You can increase **tension**. You can even tell a story.

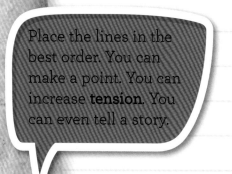

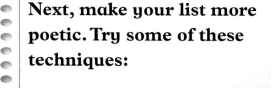

Next, make your list more poetic. Try some of these techniques:

- Add **imagery**, or figurative language. What do the list items remind you of? Compare them to other objects.
- Liven up the language. Add interesting sounds. Find words that are fun to say.
- Play with words and their meanings. Add **puns** or nonsense words.

See the Poetry Pointers all through this book for more help.

Five Steps to Writing

1. Pre-writing: Brainstorm new ideas. Write every one down, even if it seems as though it might not work.

2. Drafting: Your first copy can be sloppy. You can always fix it later.

3. Revising: Use input from other writers to make your poem better.

4. Editing: Check spelling, grammar, and punctuation.

5. Publishing: Print and distribute your poem, give it as a gift, or publish it online.

About This Book

In this book, you'll learn about one kind of poem: the list poem.

Literature Links explore the tools that all types of literature use.

Poetry Pointers explain the parts that are special to poetry.

Thinking Aloud sections include discussion questions, brainstorming tips, graphic organizers, and examples of students' writing.

Now It's Your Turn! gives you tips on how to write your very own list poems.

Chapter 2: Writing a Definition List Poem

A **definition** explains what a word means. In this chapter, you will read, recite, and write a definition list poem. Your poem can be serious or silly. It can use examples, like the poem below.

Arithmetic

Arithmetic is where numbers fly like pigeons in and out of your head.
Arithmetic tells you how many you lose or win if you know how
      many you had before you lost or won.
Arithmetic is seven eleven all good children go to heaven — or five six
      bundle of sticks.
Arithmetic is numbers you squeeze from your head to your hand to
      your pencil to your paper till you get the answer.
Arithmetic is where the answer is right and everything is nice
      and you can look out of the window and see the blue sky — or the answer is
      wrong and you have to start all over and try again and see how it
      comes out this time.
If you take a number and double it and double it again and then
      double it a few more times, the number gets bigger and bigger and goes
      higher and higher and only arithmetic can tell you what the number is when
      you decide to quit doubling.
Arithmetic is where you have to multiply — and you carry the
      multiplication table in your head and hope you won't lose it.
If you have two animal crackers, one good and one bad, and you
      eat one and a striped zebra with streaks all over him eats the other, how
      many animal crackers will you have if somebody offers you
      five six seven and you say No no no and you say Nay nay nay and you say
      Nix nix nix?
If you ask your mother for one fried egg for breakfast and she
      gives you two fried eggs and you eat both of them, who is better in
      arithmetic, you or your mother?

—Carl Sandburg

Poetry Pointer: Line Breaks

The lines in list poems can be long or short. Poets often **break**, or end, lines where a reader would take a breath. You can also end a line at the end of a phrase or thought. A line that ends with punctuation is called **end-stopped**.

You can break one thought into several lines. The poet did that in "Arithmetic." Carrying a thought from one line to the next is called **enjambment**.

The word at the end of a line gets the most attention. The word at the beginning gets the second most. You can break a line at any point you choose.

Literature Link: Similes

One way to create a clear image is to use a comparison. You can make up a **simile**. A simile compares one thing to another using the words *like* or *as*. In "Arithmetic," the comparison "numbers fly like pigeons in and out of your head" is a simile. Here are more examples:

glows like a firefly

as round as a basketball

as tiny as a crumb

Thinking Aloud

Hunter's group thought about words they could define in their poems. They wrote one list of **nouns**. Nouns name people, places, and things. They made another list of **verbs**, or action words. Here are their lists:

	Nouns	Verbs
at home	table, chair, spoon, fork, plate, house, floor, ceiling, porch, bed, lamp, TV, door, window, dog, cat, rat, snake, shoe, sock, pants, shirt	talk, listen, think, cook, bake, eat, sleep, dream, watch, play, study, hug, relax
in school	clock, desk, paper, pencil, pen, book, computer, mouse	learn, recite, ask, answer, brainstorm, write, revise
outside	crow, squirrel, bear, plane, bus, train, garden, park, city, street, lake, cricket, ant, bee	hike, run, climb, skate, float, swim, sing, dance, shop

Write Your Own Definition List Poem

When you write your definition list poem, follow these tips:

- Look up the meaning of the word in a dictionary.
- A **synonym** is a word with the same or a similar meaning. You might find one in a **thesaurus**.
- Add examples to make your definition clearer. Examples can also make your poem more interesting.
- Does your word relate to a time or place? If not, "when" and "where" usually do not belong in the definition.

Hunter wrote this poem about his favorite time of year:

Summer Vacation

Summer vacation is going barefoot
     going swimming
     going to the playground with my new baby brother
Summer vacation is watching fireworks
     watching a parade
     watching clouds from a blanket in the yard
     watching stars from a blanket in the yard
     watching my new baby brother on a blanket in the yard
Summer vacation is taking a hike
     taking a bike ride
     taking care of my new baby brother
I love summer vacation.
I love my new baby brother!

Now It's Your Turn!

Choose a word from the students' list or a word of your own. You can choose a word you want to know instead of one you already know. Look up the meaning and think of examples. Brainstorm a list of ideas. What ties everything together?

Chapter 3: Writing a Rhyming List Poem

Rhyme can make a poem more fun to read and write. It can also be a challenge! But you'll find some help here. In this chapter, you will read, recite, and write a rhyming list poem.

Miss T.

It's a very odd thing—
    As odd as can be—
That whatever Miss T. eats
    Turns into Miss T.;
Porridge and apples,
    Mince, muffins and mutton,
Jam, junket, jumbles—
    Not a rap, not a button
It matters; the moment
    They're out of her plate,
Though shared by Miss Butcher
    And sour Mr. Bate;
Tiny and cheerful,
    And neat as can be,
Whatever Miss T. eats
    Turns into Miss T.

—Walter De La Mare

Poetry Pointer: Rhyme

Listen for rhyme. You can hear it. Rhyming words sound different at the beginning. They sound alike at the end. What matters is the way the words are pronounced, not the way they are spelled. In "Miss T.," the rhyming words fall at the end of every other line. *Be* rhymes with *T.*, *mutton* rhymes with *button*, and so on.

How can you find rhyming words? A **rhyming dictionary** can help you. It doesn't tell you what a word means. It shows you a list of words that rhyme. But don't choose a word just because it rhymes. It has to make sense in your poem. Rhyming works best if you know what you want to say first. Then look for the right words to express your ideas.

?

Are you having trouble finding a rhyme that works? Try to reword the other line in the pair.

Literature Link: Alliteration

Notice how the letter *M* repeats in the line "Mince, muffins and mutton." Several words in a series begin with the same sound. (Look for a repeating letter in the next line, too!) This pattern is called **alliteration**. Here are some more examples:

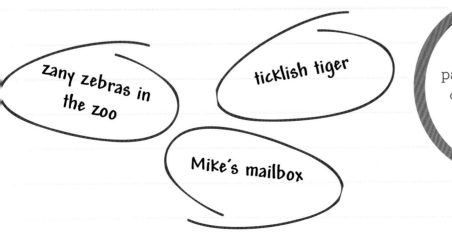

zany zebras in the zoo

ticklish tiger

Mike's mailbox

Alliteration is a pleasant pattern to hear. You can use it in your poem, too!

Thinking Aloud

Abby's group thought of things to write about. They talked about different kinds of things. They thought of things to do, things to eat, and so on. They used a **cluster** to brainstorm. They wrote the word "things" in the center and circled it. Next, the group added some different kinds of things that could become lists for their poems. Then, they added items of each kind. They circled each word or phrase and linked related ideas. Here is their cluster:

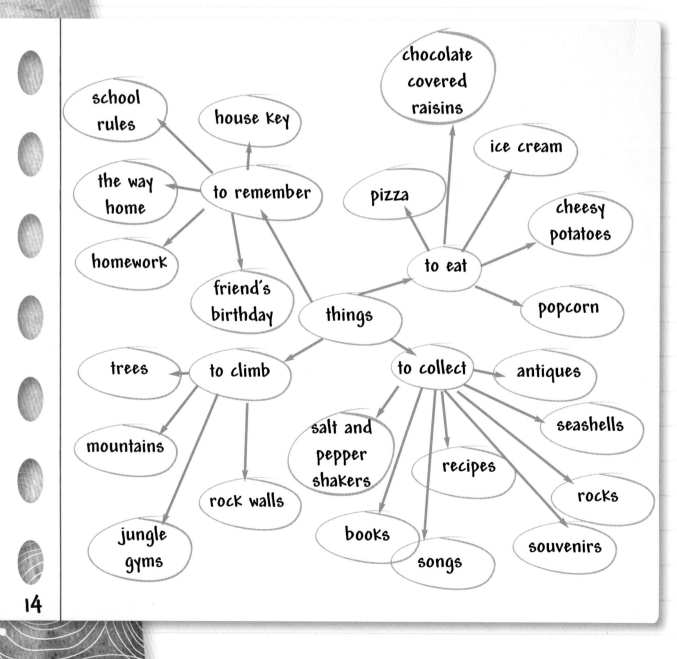

Write Your Own Rhyming List Poem

Abby is a fan of words. She wrote a rhyming list poem about some of her favorites. Here is her poem:

Words, Words, Words

I like the sound of *hoopla*.
Mishmash is fun to say.
Barracuda, bric-a-brac—
I try to find a way
to use one of my favorite words
every single day.
Morning glory, chifferobe,
gigantic, popinjay,
conundrum, hopple popple—
I'm a master of wordplay!

Now It's Your Turn!

You can choose an idea from the students' cluster for your rhyming list poem. You can let the cluster inspire you to think of something else, or create a new category if you like. You could list your favorite things to do or list questions you would like to ask. You could also list things people throw away. How about places you would like to visit?

You can use a rhyming dictionary to help you find words that rhyme. Find one at the library or on the Internet. Just be sure to say what you mean in your poem. Don't let the words lead you away from what you want to say.

15

Chapter 4: Writing a Biopoem

In this chapter, you will read, recite, and write a biopoem. A biopoem is a biography poem. It describes a person's life. You can write one about yourself or about someone else.

Many different forms of biopoems are used in schools. Some of them require you to fill in the blanks. They might create lists that are not quite poems. Look for ways to add extra details or use poetic language and techniques. Here is one form and an example that uses it:

Name	JoAnn Early Macken
(three adjectives)	Hopeful, hardworking, musical
(family relationship)	One of seven sisters; has a twin
Who loves...	Who loves poetry, canoe trips, and gardening
Who hates...	Who hates green peppers, cold weather, and wearing hats
Who wants...	Who wants to light up this poem with fireworks of words
Who wishes...	Who wishes everyone would work to understand each other
Who fears...	Who fears high places, climate change, and pesticides
Who dreams of...	Who dreams of beekeeping and raising monarch butterflies
Who wonders...	Who wonders "what if?" when she writes
Who cares about...	Who cares about clean air and water
Who lives...	Who lives in Wisconsin near a Great Lake
Name	JoAnn Early Macken

Poetry Pointer: Word Choice

Make your poem more interesting than a list. To paint a clear picture, use specific words. Listen to the **rhythm**. The rhythm is a regular pattern of stressed **syllables**. It's similar to the beat in music. Use poetic language! Here are some tips you can try:

tip	definition	examples
use a **metaphor**	a comparison that does not use the words *like* or *as*	The highway was a parking lot. The lawn is a soft carpet.
use **onomatopoeia**	a word that sounds like what it means	buzz, hum, squeak, pow
use a **symbol**	an object that stands in for something	flag, stop sign, bald eagle, badge

Literature Link: Adjectives

Words that describe nouns are called **adjectives**. In a sentence, an adjective usually comes before the noun. Here are some examples:

Adjective	Noun
hazy	sky
wet	umbrella
warm	sweater
heavy	package
messy	desk

Thinking Aloud

Jacob's group discussed the people they could write about. Here are some ideas you might want to use.

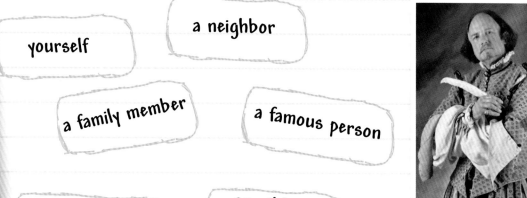

yourself

a neighbor

a family member

a famous person

a favorite author, artist, or musician

an athlete or sports hero

a historical figure

They talked about interviewing someone to find out about that person. They decided they could ask a question to learn the answer to each phrase that starts a line in their biopoem.

They thought of some other ways they could describe people. Here are some more possible line starters:

Who feels . . .

Who learned . . .

Who wants to visit . . .

Who discovered . . .

Who is proud of . . .

Who remembers . . .

Write Your Own Biopoem

Who would you like to write about? How could you describe that person? Jacob wrote this poem about himself. He used alliteration to liven up the sounds in his poem.

Jacob
Who is friendly, funny, and fearless
Who has the same name as his father
Who loves skateboarding, video games, and pizza
Who hates falling down, scraped knees, and homework
Who wants to visit the Grand Canyon
Who wishes he could whistle
Who is proud of his skateboarding skills
Who dreams of summer and long, smooth sidewalks
Who lives on a busy, noisy block
Who? Jacob!

Now It's Your Turn!

Be creative! You can change the line starters like Jacob did. Or skip one that doesn't apply. Add something else if it makes more sense. Make up your own line starters if you like. What is important about the person you chose?

If you don't know a person well, find out what you need to know first. Be sure to use reliable sources, especially if you research them online. If you interview someone, format the answers in a list. Put it in an order that makes sense. Then look for ways to make the language exciting.

Chapter 5: Writing an Acrostic

In this chapter, you will read, recite, and write an acrostic. In an acrostic, one letter in each line spells a word or phrase when read down the page. Usually, that letter is first in each line. Sometimes it is last or in the middle.

Lewis Carroll wrote *Alice's Adventures in Wonderland*. He also wrote this poem. The first letter in each line spells the name of his young friend, Alice Pleasance Liddell.

A Boat, Beneath a Sunny Sky

A boat, beneath a sunny sky
Lingering onward dreamily
In an evening of July—

Children three that nestle near,
Eager eye and willing ear,
Pleased a simple tale to hear—

Long has paled that sunny sky:
Echoes fade and memories die:
Autumn frosts have slain July.

Still she haunts me, phantomwise,
Alice moving under skies
Never seen by waking eyes.

Children yet, the tale to hear,
Eager eye and willing ear,
Lovingly shall nestle near.

In a Wonderland they lie,
Dreaming as the days go by,
Dreaming as the summers die:

Ever drifting down the stream—
Lingering in the golden gleam—
Life, what is it but a dream?

—Lewis Carroll

Poetry Pointer: Stanzas

"A Boat, Beneath a Sunny Sky" is broken into groups of three lines. These groups are called **stanzas**. Stanzas in poems are like paragraphs in prose. A poem with more than one idea can be divided into two or more stanzas.

Some acrostics use more than one vertical word. Each word can form a separate stanza. Carroll could have divided this poem into three stanzas. He could have started one with *Alice*, one with *Pleasance*, and one with *Liddell*. Instead, he chose to break the poem into seven stanzas of three lines each.

Literature Link: Repetition

To repeat something means to do or say it more than once. Repeating a word, a phrase, or a line can help make a point.

What does repetition add to this poem?

In "A Boat, Beneath a Sunny Sky," the word *dream* (and variations of it) appears four times. Can you spot all four? One whole line is repeated. Can you find it? Which other words repeat?

dream
dream
dream
dream

Thinking Aloud

The word or phrase from which you build your acrostic is important. It gives you the topic. But some letters (such as J, Q, X, and Z) might be harder to work with. Focus on fitting logical words into place.

Mara's group wondered which words they could use to begin their lines. They brainstormed these ideas:

your name

the name of a family member or friend

a famous person's name

the name of your school

your school team or mascot

a motto or common saying

your pet's name

your city, state, or country

a hobby

a favorite word or phrase

a secret wish

a goal

Write Your Own Acrostic

Lewis Carroll wrote in rhyme. But you don't have to!
Mara wrote about her cat. To add interest to her poem,
she repeated a line. She added alliteration, too.

Snuggles in my lap
A fine feline friend
Meows when I walk in the door
A fine feline friend
Nudges me with her nose
Tickles me with her whiskers
Howls when she is hungry
A fine feline friend

Now It's Your Turn!

You might be tempted to start by filling in
words with the letters you are looking for. If
you do, you could miss an important thought.
First, brainstorm good ideas or gather the
details you need. Then look for ways to make
those points in your poem. Capitalize the letters
in your vertical word. That makes it stand out
and easier to see.

Chapter 6: Writing a Riddle Poem

In this chapter, you will read, recite, and write a riddle poem. A riddle poem might present a puzzle to solve. It might ask a question. Some riddle poems include the answer within the poem. Others, like these examples, reveal it after the end.

I paint without colors, I fly without wings,
I people the air with most fanciful things;
I hear sweetest music where no sound is heard,
And eloquence moves me, nor utters a word.
The past and the present together I bring,
The distant and near gather under my wing.
Far swifter than lightning my wonderful flight,
Through the sunshine of day, or the darkness of night;
And those who would find me, must find me, indeed,
As this picture they scan, and this poesy read.

—Author Unknown

(Answer: imagination)

? Compare the two poems. What is similar? What is different?

The beginning of eternity,
The end of time and space,
The beginning of every end,
The end of every race?

—Author Unknown

(Answer: the letter E)

Poetry Pointer: Personification

In the first riddle poem example, the poet writes about imagination as though it is alive. It paints, it flies, it hears, and so on. This is called **personification**. You can use personification, too. You can write about a nonliving object as though it is alive. You can also write about an animal or object as though it is a person.

Literature Link: Point of View

Who will speak in your poem?

That voice shows the **point of view**.

First person: The speaker in the poem uses *I, me,* or *we.* (The first example poem uses first person. Your poem can, too. But the "I" in the poem does not really have to be you. You can pretend to be someone or something else.)

Second person: The speaker in the poem speaks to someone or something. It can use *you,* either singular or plural.

Third person: The speaker in the poem talks about someone or something. It uses *he, she, it,* or *they.* (That's everyone except *you* and *me.*) You don't see the word *it* in the second example poem. But it uses third person.

Are you trying to show more than one perspective in your poem? If not, the point of view should stay the same through the entire poem.

25

Thinking Aloud

Matt's group talked about objects to write riddle poems about. They wanted hints that were not too easy and not too hard. Here are some of their ideas:

Object	Hint
needle	I have one eye. Look for me in a haystack.
scissors	Your fingers fit into my handles. I click when I work.
window	You can see inside or outside through me.
flashlight	Carry me with you in the dark. I'm perfect for camping.
string	You can tie me in knots. I hold things together.
road	I'm a long, paved path to somewhere else.
key	I open a door, a diary, or a suitcase.
caterpillar	I crawl, I wriggle, I wait to grow wings.
doorbell	I announce visitors.
ice skates	We glide on shimmering surfaces.
backpack	I'm a convenient carryall.
wave	I crash on the beach. I flow in and out.
calendar	I divide the year into pages.

Write Your Own Riddle Poem

Matt wrote this riddle poem. See if you can guess the answer before you read the last line!

I whoosh.
I whisper.
I roar.
I steal hats and turn umbrellas inside out.
I move seeds from place to place.
I lift your kite.
I make trees shake.
What am I? I am the wind.

Now It's Your Turn!

To write your own riddle poem, choose an object to write about. (You can use one of the ideas in the students' list if you like.) Brainstorm a list of actions and descriptions that fit the object. You can put the answer inside the poem or after it.

In the next chapter, you will read about how other students helped Matt revise his poem.

Chapter 7: Revising Your List Poem

Congratulations! You have just completed the first two steps of writing. You brainstormed new ideas. You used them to write your first draft. Now you are ready for the next two steps: revising and editing. Use this checklist as a guide:

Yes/No	List Poem Revision Checklist
	Did you choose the most important items for your list?
	Did you choose the best clues or details?
	Are the items in your list all connected?
	Did you use poetic techniques?
	Are the line breaks in logical places?

Group Help

One good way to revise your poem is to share it with a group. Give each person a copy. Ask them to write their comments on it. Ask one person to read your poem aloud. Listen for any places where the reader stumbles. Give the others a chance to speak before you say anything about your work.

Then move to the next writing step. Did they see anything you need to edit? Are there any spelling, grammar, or punctuation errors to correct?

Take time to think about every comment. Try the ones that make the most sense to you.

Matt's group liked his riddle poem. Hunter thought Matt could break line 4 into two lines. Abby said Matt could change *lift* to *carry*. Jacob suggested changing *move* to a more active verb. Mara thought that Matt should arrange the order of the lines from calm to stormy. Matt also changed *shake* to *tremble*. Here is his revised poem:

I whisper.
I whoosh.
I roar.
I carry your kite.
I steal your hat.
I turn your umbrella inside out.
I whisk seeds from place to place.
I make trees tremble.
What am I? I am the wind.

Helping others revise and edit their poems can help you, too. When you read others' work, look for positive parts. Point out what works well. Be supportive. Writing is not easy. Sharing can be even harder! If you don't understand something, ask a question.

Chapter 8: Performing a Poem

The final step of writing is publishing your work. After you finish the final copy of your poem, share it with others. You can read your poem aloud to a group. You can read alone or as a **chorus**. If you have a dramatic flair, perform your own poem!

First, practice reading your poem aloud.

> Speak slowly.

> Speak clearly.

> Read with feeling.

Did your group write riddle poems? Take turns reading them aloud. See who can guess the answers. You could even dress up for your roles.

Biopoems can be part of celebrations. Share each student's biopoem on his or her birthday. Did you write about a famous person? Read your biopoem on a holiday. (Make one up if you want!)

Did you write an acrostic? Make a poster of the poem. Listeners can read along and see the structure.

When others are reading, be a good audience. Listen to the speaker. Applaud at the end. Enjoy the show!

Learning More

Books

African Acrostics: A Word in Edgeways by Avis Harley. Candlewick Press (2012)

Butterfly Eyes and Other Secrets of the Meadow by Joyce Sidman. HMH Books for Young Readers (2006)

Spot the Plot: A Riddle Book of Book Riddles by J. Patrick Lewis. Chronicle Books (2009)

When Riddles Come Rumbling: Poems to Ponder by Rebecca Kai Dotlich. WordSong (2013)

Write a Poem Step by Step by JoAnn Early Macken. Earlybird Press (2012)

Websites

From Kenn Nesbitt:

How to Write an Acrostic:
www.poetry4kids.com/blog/lessons/how-to-write-an-acrostic-poem/

How to Write a Funny List Poem:
www.poetry4kids.com/blog/lessons/how-to-write-a-funny-list-poem/

Writing Riddle Rhymes: www.poetry4kids.com/blog/news/writing-riddles/

"Where I'm From" (another kind of autobiographical poem) by George Ella Lyon: www.georgeellalyon.com/where.html

Write a List Poem (Amy Ludwig VanDerwater): www.poemfarm.amylv.com/2011/04/write-list-poem.html

Glossary

Note: Some boldfaced words are defined where they appear in the book.

chorus A group of people who sing or speak something together

cluster A brainstorming technique that links related words together

imagery Descriptive language that makes readers imagine pictures

personification Describing an animal or object as though it is a person or a nonliving object as though it is alive

phrase A short group of words

point of view The speaker's position in relation to the story being told

pun A humorous use of a word or words; wordplay

rhyme Identical sounds at the ends of words

rhythm A pattern of regular sounds in a series of words

stanza A group of lines in a poem

syllable One of the parts into which a word is divided when it is pronounced

tension A feeling of excitement or fear created in a poem or story

thesaurus A book with lists of words that have similar meanings

Index